The Way of St. James

Step by Step

33 Day Devotional and Journal

Mary Maddox

Kathleen Aparo

Prayerful Path

Walking the Way of St. James, Step by Step, 33 Day Devotional and Journal. Copyright © 2018 Mary Maddox/Kathleen Aparo. No part of this book may be used or reproduced in any manner without written permission except in brief quotations.

All rights reserved.

Prayerful Path

Guided and self guided pilgrimages offered. For more information. www.prayerfulpath.com prayerfulpath@gmail.com

ISBN-10: 1985017938
ISBN-13: 978-1985017931

DEDICATION

For the many pilgrims who have embarked on this journey for the soul.

A Prayer for Pilgrims

God, who brought your servant Abraham out of the land of the Chaldeans, protecting him in his wanderings, who guided the Hebrew people across the desert, we ask that you watch over us, your servants, as we walk in the love of your name to the shrine of St. James, Santiago de Compostela.

Be for us our companion on the walk,
Our guide at the crossroads,
Our breath in our weariness,
Our protection in danger,
Our home along the way,
Our shade in the heat,
Our light in the darkness,
Our consolation in our discouragements,
And our strength in our intentions.

With your guidance may we arrive safe and sound at the end of our journey, and, enriched with grace and virtue. May we return safely to our homes filled with joy.

We make this prayer in faith.

St. James, pray for us.
Holy Mary, pray for us.

Rituals and Traditions of the Camino de Santiago

> *"Give me my scallop-shell of quiet, My staff of faith to walk upon, My scrip of joy, immortal diet, My bottle of Salvation, My gown of glory (hope's true gage), And then I'll take my Pilgrimage."*
> ~Sir Walter Raleigh, The Passionate Man's Pilgrimage, 1603

During medieval times, the pilgrims who were making their way to Santiago de Compostela established many traditions and rituals. Today there are thousands who still follow some of these traditions. Perhaps in these rituals they feel the powerful prayers of faith and courage passed down by those who walked before them on this Camino. Certainly, take upon yourselves whatever tradition or ritual that feeds your soul. It can only enhance your journey.

Here is a ritual done before you embark on your Camino. In the past, a pilgrim would have been granted permission to leave by his local religious authority. Dressed in his pilgrim clothes with his staff and scrip (a small medieval bag used to carry food, money, etc.) and after taking an oath to remain loyal to his monarch, he would ask for a blessing from his local priest. Then and only then would he set off on his journey.

STEP BY STEP

Today, we don't need permission, but a blessing is a wonderful way to begin your pilgrimage. Speak to your priest or a faith filled friend and ask for a blessing on your upcoming Camino. Some pilgrim organizations offer these blessings. So, don't be shy; go forward and ask for the gift of a blessing. And remember, your pilgrimage begins the moment you cross the threshold of your front door.

TRADITIONS AND RITUALS ...

- As you pass a pilgrim along the Camino, these are the greetings that are used: "buen camino" in Spain, "bon chemin" in France, and "bom caminho" in Portugal.

- The history of the Camino shell and why it symbolizes being a pilgrim: In and around 1100, pilgrimages were long and dangerous journeys. These pilgrimages were undertaken as an act of penance and religious devotion. When pilgrims returned home, they presented the scallop shell as proof they completed the pilgrimage because the shells were indigenous to the Galician coast. By the 12th Century, scallop shells were being sold by hundreds of licensed vendors around the Cathedral of Santiago. This cemented their symbolic status.

- One important monastery among the Camino was in San Salvador. The monks at the monastery would ring the bell to help guide the pilgrims across the Pyrenees in bad weather.

- In Triacastela, the earliest pilgrims were given a piece of limestone to carry to Castanola to a lime-making works. Lime from there was used in the building of the cathedral of Santiago de Compostela.

- There are many churches where the pilgrims would worship. They would pray to the particular saint associated with the Chapel, asking the Saint to pray for them and their intentions. This practice continues today. As you walk your journey along the Camino, visit the churches. Take a moment; remember this is not a race. Sit in silence. Quiet yourself and feel all the prayers said before you in this little piece of beauty. *St. James, pray for us.*

- In Estella, you can pray to the Virgin of El Puy. The legend says that a group of shepherds were guided to a cave by a downfall of many stars. They entered the cave and found an image of the Virgin on the cave walls. They rushed to tell the priest. When they returned with the priest, they tried to move the image of the Virgin. The image could not be moved. A divine force kept the image in that place and a shrine was then built around the image. In 1090 the king of Navarre, Sancho Ramirez, founded the town of Estella. Due to the large numbers of pilgrims on the Camino de Santiago, Estella became an important town, providing protection and giving shelter to the many pilgrims. *Virgin of El Puy, pray for us.*

STEP BY STEP

- Continuing on to just outside of Estrella, take advantage of a ritual added in modern times. Make sure you take a sip of Rioja wine at the wine fountain of Bodegas Irache.

- In Leon at the Cathedral, the pilgrims would rub their hands on the column bearing the statue of St James dressed in pilgrim garb.

- The Iron Cross or Cruz de Ferro has several theories about it, but only one ritual. Some claim that the cross was erected to guide pilgrims, especially in the winter months, when the route can be obscured by snow. Others suggest that the cross originates from Roman times marking the border between territories. However, since the 11th century, the cross has been an important monument on the Camino de Santiago. Pilgrims traditionally carry a stone with them from the start of their journey. The rock symbolizes the sins that the pilgrim has committed and the guilt and the burdens we all carry in life. By leaving a stone his stone, the pilgrim was leaving behind his sin, his guilt, his shame, and his burdens, thus walking more lightly onto Santiago, absolved of his mistakes in life.

Take a moment here, leave your stone, pause and pray at this humble monument.

- Nearing Santiago, the pilgrims would stop in the town of Lavacolla. There they would bathe in the river before entering the city, washing away the dust and dirt from their time on the Camino. We may not bathe in the river, but we can take a moment and say a prayer of thanksgiving.

- Not too far up the road is Mount Gozo, called the Mount of Joy. From the top of the mountain, you will be able to see the spires of the Cathedral in Santiago. This is the first time you will see the Cathedral. The pilgrims would race to the summit. Whoever saw the towers first cried out, "Mon Joie!" He was then considered "king" of the group. Mount Gozo is a very emotional experience. This is your moment. Follow your heart; pray, sing, dance, stand in awe or do all of the above. This is it; you now can see your destination. Santiago de Compostela!

You have made it to Santiago. Now what? Here are a few traditions everyone follows.

- On entering the cathedral and the shrine of St James, the first sight that greets you is the beautiful Portico de la Gloria, sculpted in the 12th century. Ferdinand of Leon paid Maestro Mateo a salary of two marks a week to design and carve over 185 different statues that make up the religious scenes of the gateway. This piece of medieval art is stunning.

STEP BY STEP

The entryway was created over a twenty-year period by the master sculptor Mateo, who finished the remarkable frieze in 1188.
Carved into its center column is the figure of St. James, while above him Christ sits surrounded by his disciples and dozens of other religious figures and motifs, a work one could easily spend a day contemplating (indeed, in the Middle Ages such works were said to be the Bible of the poor). ~Lori Erickson

- As a pilgrim, you will need to place your hand on the center pillar known as the Tree of Jesse. Carved into this pillar is the seated figure of St. James carrying a pilgrim's staff and a scroll which reads, "The Lord Sent Me". As you place your hands in the grooves formed by the millions of pilgrims before you, the tradition here is to say a prayer of thanksgiving or five Hail Marys for your safe arrival. Now walk to the other side of the column. There you will see a figure of a kneeling man. This is believed to be the self-portrait of the artist Maestro Mateo. To receive some of the master's wisdom and genius, you must knock your forehead three times gently on his head. The statue of Maestro Mateo is also called "The Saint of the Bumps". No need to explain why he has this nickname.

Now it is time to contemplate the interior of the cathedral.

- At the end of the long center aisle, a dazzling Baroque altar blazes with gold. It includes three depictions of St. James as teacher, pilgrim, and knight. Even with its magnificent overwhelming ornate alter it welcomes pilgrims in an intimate way.

- The pilgrims are invited to climb the stairs that lead to an area behind the altar, where they can embrace the gilded statue of St. James from behind, wrapping their arms around him in a hug. After this embrace, pilgrims descend into the crypt where the saint's relics are kept in a silver casket. Kneel and reflect on your pilgrimage. *Thank you St. James.*

On emerging from the depths, spend some time visiting the chapels around the sides of the cathedral.

> *The cathedral seems filled with the petitions of the millions of pilgrims who have journeyed here over the centuries, bringing their prayers, hopes, dreams, and pleadings for mercy. After traveling so far to arrive here, many people spend hours in contemplation in the church, clearly reluctant to end their pilgrimage.* ~ Lori Erikson

- Go to confession and attend the Pilgrim's Mass. If you are lucky, you might be able to witness the botafumeiro, a huge incensory made of silver-plated brass. This was originally used to help mask the smell of the pilgrims leaving behind a trail of smoke and the fragrance of incense. Now it is used for special occasions and services.

STEP BY STEP

- After confession and Mass pilgrims would go and get their Compostela, a letter proving completion of their pilgrimage. From the very beginning of the Camino de Santiago pilgrimages, the pilgrim would desire to be recognized in some way for completing his journey.

- For many years, the scallop shell was a symbol of arrival at the Tomb of St James. However, this simple practice was discredited as many vendors were selling the scallop shell fraudulently. This became a problem for the true pilgrim. The Church then had to impose a penalty of excommunication on the vendors who were behaving in this way. Starting in the 13th century the "evidential letters" were used as a more effective way of recording a completed pilgrimage. These are the direct roots of the Compostela.

After ten centuries, these rituals and traditions of the Camino de Santiago continue to this day. Modern-day pilgrims and visitors line up in the cathedral to place their right hands in the holes on the Tree of Jesse, bump heads with Maestro Mateo, hug the statue at the Shrine of St James, attend Mass, go to confession and wait in line for their Compostela.

Step by Step as you make your way to Santiago, enjoy these traditions, and remember Buen Camino!

Ways to enhance your steps ….

Lectio Divina:

Lectio Divina is a slow, contemplative praying of the Scriptures. Time set aside in a special way for Lectio Divina enables us to discover in our daily life an underlying spiritual rhythm. In this rhythm, offer more of yourselves and your relationships to the Father, and accept God's embrace. Choose a text of the Scriptures that you wish to pray. Allow yourself to become silent. Focus on your breathing, find a mantra - whatever is best for you. Give yourself time to enjoy the silence for a few moments.

> *Read it slowly, gently. Savor each portion of the reading, constantly listening for the "still, small voice" of a word or phrase that somehow says, "I am for you today." Do not expect lightning or ecstasies. In lectio divina, God is teaching us to listen to him, to seek him in silence. He does not reach out and grab us; rather, he gently invites us ever more deeply into his presence. Take that word or phrase into yourself. Memorize it and slowly repeat it to yourself, allowing it to interact with your inner world of concerns, memories, and ideas. Do not be afraid of distractions. Memories or thoughts are simply parts of yourself that, when they*

STEP BY STEP

> *rise up during lectio divina, are asking to be given to God along with the rest of your inner self. Allow this inner pondering, this rumination, to invite you into dialogue with God. ~ Father Luke Dysinger, OSB*

Now step by step, walk in prayer for the day with that word or phrase.

> *Speak to God. Whether you use words, ideas, or images--or all three--is not important. Interact with God as you would with one who you know loves and accepts you. And give to him what you have discovered during your experience of meditation. Experience God by using the word or phrase he has given you as a means of blessing and of transforming the ideas and memories that your reflection on his word has awakened. Give to God what you have found within your heart.*

> *Rest in God's embrace. And when he invites you to return to your contemplation of his word or to your inner dialogue with him, do so. Learn to use words when words are helpful, and to let go of words when they no longer are necessary. Rejoice in the knowledge that God is with you in both words and silence, in spiritual activity and inner receptivity. ~ Father Luke Dysinger, OSB*

The Liturgy of the Hours:

The practice of praying the hours can be found throughout the Psalms. "Seven times a day I praise you" (Psalm 119:164), "At midnight I will rise and thank you," (Psalm 119:162), and "In the morning I will offer you my prayer" (Psalm 5:3).

In the sixth century, St Benedict formalized the practice by naming each hour. This has formed the basis of prayer for many monastics. Along this journey, you will have the opportunity to join the Monks in praying these prayers. You may enjoy the monastic experience of praying the hours, meditating on the divine meanings of each of the eight Hours of your day as explained here by Brother David Steindl-Rast, a Benedictine monk.

> *The Canonical hours are the seasons of the monastic day and for us to hear the music of silence, we must step out of clock time into the monastic flow of time as expressed through the hours of the day. We must forsake our usual unconscious gesture of reaction and make the aware inner gesture of response to what is before us in the moment. Monastic hours are divine messengers, everyday angels that announce the gifts and challenges of each part of the day. ~ Brother David Steindl-Rast*

Walking Meditation:

I can't think of a better way to bring mindfulness practice into our body and into the outside world than through walking, strolling, or rolling at one to three miles an hour. It changes everything. It trains us, both on the inside and the outside, to begin seeing God, the Great Spirit, in ourselves and in others in such foundational ways. This humble posture invites us into the fragile details behind our own breath, the curious creatures high in the trees, and the struggle in being a pedestrian in today's time. Mindful walking can invite new ideas, new ways of seeing, and new ways of understanding with every step. ~ Jonathon Stalls, "What Really Frightens Us?"

When we practice [mindfulness], we are liberated from fear, sorrow, and the fires burning inside of us. When mindfulness embraces our joy, our sadness, and all our other mental formations, sooner or later we will see their deep roots. With every mindful step and every mindful breath, we see the roots of our mental formations. Mindfulness shines its light upon them and helps them to transform. Thich Nhat Hanh, The Heart of the Buddha's Teaching (Berkeley: Broadway Books, 1999), 75

Step by step walk mindfully, present to God's presence.

The Rosary:

In the spiritual journey of the Rosary, based on the constant contemplation – in Mary's company – of the face of Christ, this demanding ideal of being conformed to him is pursued through an association which could be described in terms of friendship. We are thereby enabled to enter naturally into Christ's life and as it were to share his deepest feelings. In this regard Blessed Bartolo Longo has written: "Just as two friends, frequently in each other's company, tend to develop similar habits, so too, by holding familiar converse with Jesus and the Blessed Virgin, by meditating on the mysteries of the Rosary and by living the same life in Holy Communion, we can become, to the extent of our lowliness, similar to them and can learn from these supreme models a life of humility, poverty, hiddenness, patience and perfection. ~St. John Paul II

The mysteries of the Rosary:

These days are suggested just to help us, but you can pray whichever mystery you are being called to pray!

Mondays and Saturdays: The Joyful Mysteries remind the faithful of Christ's birth: The Annunciation (Luke 1:26–38); The Visitation (Luke 1:39–56); The Nativity (Luke 2:1–21); The Presentation (Luke 2:22–38); The Finding of the Child Jesus in the Temple (Luke 2:41–52)

Tuesdays and Fridays: The Sorrowful Mysteries recall Jesus' passion and death: The Agony of Jesus in the Garden (Matthew 26:36–56); The Scourging at the Pillar (Matthew

27:26); The Crowning with Thorns (Matthew 27:27–31); The Carrying of the Cross (Matthew 27:32); The Crucifixion (Matthew 27:33–56).

Wednesdays and Sundays: The Glorious Mysteries focus on the resurrection of Jesus and the glories of heaven: The Resurrection (John 20:1–29); The Ascension (Luke 24:36–53); The Descent of the Holy Spirit (Acts 2:1–41); The Assumption of Mary, the Mother of God, into heaven; The Coronation of Mary in heaven.

Thursdays: Pope John Paul II added The Mysteries of Light, also known as the Luminous Mysteries, in 2002: The Baptism in the River Jordan (Matthew 3:13–16); The Wedding Feast at Cana (John 2:1–11); The Preaching of the coming of the Kingdom of God (Mark 1:14–15); The Transfiguration (Matthew 17:1–8); The Institution of the Holy Eucharist (Matthew 26).

The prayers of the Rosary:

Apostles' Creed, The Crucifix: I believe in God, the Father Almighty, Creator of Heaven and earth; and in Jesus Christ, His only Son, Our Lord, Who was conceived by the Holy Spirit, born of the Virgin Mary, suffered under Pontius Pilate, was crucified; died, and was buried. He descended into Hell; the third day He arose again from the dead; He ascended into Heaven, sits at the right hand of God, the Father Almighty; from thence He shall come to judge the living and the dead. I believe in the Holy Spirit, the holy Catholic Church, the communion of saints, the forgiveness of sins, the resurrection of the body, and life everlasting. Amen.

Our Father, Single Beads: Our Father, Who art in heaven, hallowed be Thy name; Thy kingdom come; Thy will be done on earth as it is in heaven. Give us this day our daily bread; and forgive us our trespasses as we forgive those who trespass against us; and lead us not into temptation, but deliver us from evil, Amen.

Hail Mary, 10 beads: Hail Mary, full of grace. The Lord is with thee. Blessed art thou among women, and blessed is the fruit of thy womb, Jesus. Holy Mary, Mother of God, pray for us sinners, now and at the hour of our death. Amen.

Glory Be, at the end of the Hail Marys: Glory be to the Father, to the Son, and to the Holy Spirit, as it was in the beginning, is now, and ever shall be, world without end. Amen.

Fatima Prayer after the Glory Be: O My Jesus, forgive us our sins, save us from the fires of hell and lead all souls to heaven, especially those in most need of Thy mercy. Amen.

At the end of your Rosary, say the Hail Holy Queen and the following:

Hail, Holy Queen, Mother of mercy, our life, our sweetness, and our hope. To thee do we cry, poor banished children of Eve, to thee do we send up our sighs, mourning and weeping in this valley of tears. Turn then, most gracious advocate, thine eyes of mercy toward us; and after this our exile show unto us the blessed fruit of thy womb Jesus, O clement, O loving, O sweet Virgin Mary. Pray for us, O holy Mother of God. That we may be made worthy of the promises of Christ.

STEP BY STEP

Let us pray,

O God, whose only-begotten Son, by His life, death, and resurrection, has purchased for us the rewards of eternal salvation; grant we beseech Thee, that meditating upon these mysteries of the most holy Rosary of the Blessed Virgin Mary, we may imitate what they contain and obtain what they promise. Through the same Christ our Lord. Amen.

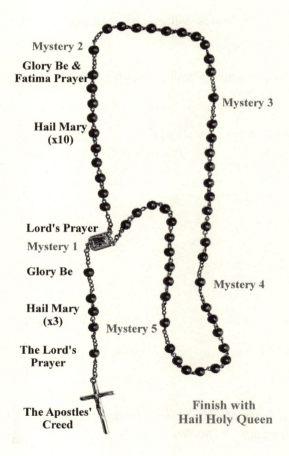

Your thoughts before you start ...

What are the dates of your Camino?

Where will you start your Camino?

How many miles will you be walking?

Who will you be walking with?

Do you have any special intentions/prayers/thoughts for your Camino?

"A journey of a thousand miles begins with a single step." ~ Lao Tzu

STEP BY STEP

Your thoughts before you start ...

"Life with Christ is a wonderful adventure."
~ Pope St. John Paul II

Day 1

His mercies are new every morning

> With every breath I take today, I vow to be awake;
>
> And every step I take, I vow to take with a grateful heart...
>
> So I may see with eyes of love into the hearts of all I meet,
>
> To ease their burden when I can and touch them with a smile. ~ Buddhist Prayer

To be grateful, to look through the eyes of love into the hearts of others and to ease another's burden with a smile, takes not a word. All it takes is to be unafraid to be awake to the God in you. Changed by it and then brave enough to face the world.

STEP BY STEP

Your thoughts ...

"Nothing glows brighter than the heart awakened to the light of love that lives within it." —Guy Finley

Day 2

And then there is Mary

This journey of faith cannot be taken without looking at Jesus' mother, Mary. Why?

Because every strength we need, all the courage we need, the faith we need, shines through her life. She said "yes" to an angel and didn't ask anyone to help her make that decision. She had courage. She courageously told her parents what the angel asked of her, risking their questions and disbelief. She had strength. She told Joseph her story, knowing he would find it hard to believe and may, in his sorrow and anger, leave her. She had faith. And because she is so loved by our God, he gives her a direct line to us.

Ask her to guide you, to strengthen you, to fill your heart with trust in God.

> *Hail Mary, full of Grace, the Lord is with Thee.*
> *Blessed art thou among women*
> *and blessed is the fruit of thy womb, Jesus.*
> *Holy Mary mother of God, pray for us sinners,*
> *now and at the hour of our death, Amen.*

Repeat, repeat, and repeat for peace of mind.

STEP BY STEP

Your thoughts ...

Blessed are you, pilgrim, if you discover that the "camino" opens your eyes to what is not seen. ~ Beatitudes of the pilgrim

Day 3

Walking in Beauty: Navajo Way Blessing

Today I will walk out, today everything evil will leave me,
I will be as I was before, I will have a cool breeze over my body.
I will have a light body, I will be happy forever, nothing will hinder me.
I walk with beauty before me. I walk with beauty behind me.
I walk with beauty below me. I walk with beauty above me.
I walk with beauty around me. My words will be beautiful.

In beauty all day long may I walk.
Through the returning seasons, may I walk.
On the trail marked with pollen may I walk.
With dew about my feet, may I walk.

With beauty before me may I walk.
With beauty behind me may I walk.
With beauty below me may I walk.
With beauty above me may I walk.
With beauty all around me may I walk.

In old age wandering on a trail of beauty, lively, may I walk.
In old age wandering on a trail of beauty, living again, may I walk.
My words will be beautiful.
My words will be beautiful…

STEP BY STEP

Your thoughts ...

Blessed are you, pilgrim, if what concerns you most is not to arrive, as to arrive with others. ~ Beatitudes of the pilgrim

Day 4

"For most of us the prayer in Gethsemane is the only model. Removing mountains can wait." ~C.S. Lewis

We are the most devout when we are in trouble. Crisis brings us to our knees. And like Christ in the Garden of Gethsemane, our prayers are filled with longings for relief. *"My Father, if it is possible, let this cup pass me by."* In this place, this garden, Jesus longed to be released from the cross before him. His prayers pleaded for relief. And then came his acceptance and words of deep spiritual courage. *"Still, let it be as you would have it, not as I."*

Our struggles with acceptance are divine struggles. To go on, to trust in God, to cling to His promises, is to accept our own "way of the cross." Remember Jesus went before us with those same struggles. He knows our weakness; he had his. He knows our broken hearts. *"My heart is nearly broken with sorrow,"* he tells us in Matt. 26:38. Jesus prepares us here for our own Gethsemane and then teaches us that with God's grace and wondrous mercy, our challenges can and will come through on the side of victory.

Alleluia, Alleluia

STEP BY STEP

Your thoughts ...

Blessed are you, pilgrim, when you contemplate the "camino" and you discover it is full of names and dawns. ~ Beatitudes of the pilgrim

Day 5

"When you make the Divine your source, you move through life with an ease and lightness, with an open hand. You allow whatever wishes to come, come. And whatever wishes to go, go. Every gain, and loss, has an odd kind of Providence." ~ Tosha Silver, "Outrageous Openness"

Is it "outrageous openness" to let God take the lead in our lives? If so, there are many souls who have been beautifully outrageous in that way. Jesus and all the great teachers and saints who followed - outrageous for sure. And the blessed ones who spoke up and lived their truth; Martin Luther King, Dorothy Day and St. Mother Teresa are just a few souls who lived their lives outrageously for the good. They moved through life with an open hand. Ready for the divine to take the lead. Think of the freedom of that.

STEP BY STEP

Your thoughts ...

Blessed are you, pilgrim, because you have discovered that the authentic "camino" begins when it is completed.
~ Beatitudes of the pilgrim

Day 6

"Always God is with us. And, in the long run, that is all we need to know." ~ David Watson

In the shadows of our day,

in the middle of our dark night,

amidst our dry prayers and our souls longing for peace …

Do we believe that God is with us? Or are we waiting for a grand experience to awaken us to God's presence? Don't. There is no waiting. The grand experience happened at our birth and God does not forget his children. Pray that your eyes will be open to the new horizon God is showing you. "Always, God is with us." Important words to remember.

STEP BY STEP

Your thoughts ...

Blessed are you, pilgrim, if your knapsack is emptying of things and your heart does not know where to hang up so many feelings and emotions.~ Beatitudes of the pilgrim

Day 7

"Seeing the crowds, he went onto the mountain. And when he was seated his disciples came to him. Then he began to speak. This is what he taught them: "How blessed are the poor in spirit; the kingdom of Heaven is theirs."
~Matthew 5:1-3

And so begins Jesus' teaching of The Beatitudes. He speaks to the crowd there and to us today about blessedness in every state of our being. He speaks to our sorrows, our poverty and to those unjustly persecuted and calls those sufferings "blessed." Then he looks into our hearts and sees the blessedness of us as the gentle, the merciful, the pure of heart and those who thirst for uprightness. But why is the first Beatitude about "spiritual poverty?" Fr. Richard Rohr talks about this and why it takes first place in Jesus' teaching on the mountain.

> *The gospel sense of "poverty of spirit" is the first necessary Beatitude because it allows us to join the whole human race in a willing and honest way.*

Jesus names our different places in life and then connects us, everyone, in our "blessedness." No one can escape his desire to call us blessed. No one!

STEP BY STEP

Your thoughts ...

Blessed are you, pilgrim, if you discover that one step back to help another is more valuable than a hundred forward without seeing what is at your side. ~ Beatitudes of the pilgrim

Day 8

The Sojourners Prayer – Thomas Merton

My Lord God, I have no idea where I am going. I do not see the road ahead of me. I cannot know for certain where it will end. Nor do I really know myself, and the fact that I think I am following your will does not mean that I am actually doing so. But I believe that the desire to please you does in fact please you. And I hope I have that desire in all that I am doing. I hope that I will never do anything apart from that desire. And I know that if I do this, you will lead me by the right road, though I may know nothing about it. Therefore will I trust you always though I may seem lost in the shadow of death. I will not fear, for you are ever with me, and you will never leave me to face my perils alone.

STEP BY STEP

Your thoughts ...

Blessed are you, pilgrim, when you don't have words to give thanks for everything that surprises you at every twist and turn of the way. ~ Beatitudes of the pilgrim

Day 9

"Truly you have formed my inmost being; you knit me in my mother's womb. I give you thanks that I am fearfully, wonderfully made; wonderful are your works." ~ Psalm 139: 13,14

Lord, guide me, lead me, help me to begin again the holy task of recognizing and loving my true self, the one you knit deep in my mother's womb. I am blinded by the needs of others, the sadness of life and my lack of confidence in my deep longings. Let your grace fall upon me to help me face the challenges only I have set before me. Be patient with me, Lord. And strengthen my faith. I know you are knocking on the door of my Spirit every day. I'm here Lord! I'm here! Let each step I take on this journey be a step toward "my inmost being, the one you knit in my mother's womb" all those years ago.

STEP BY STEP

Your thoughts ...

"If one completes the journey to one's own heart, one will find oneself in the heart of everyone else." ~ Father Thomas Keating

Day 10

"Ask, and it will be given to you; search and you will find; knock and the door will be opened to you. Everyone who asks receives; everyone who searches finds; everyone who knocks will have the door opened." ~ Matthew. 7:7

Jesus has said it. Ask and you will receive! Search and you shall find! Knock and the door will open! What you receive, what you find, what you see at the door is meant to move you forward; to move you forward into a world beyond ourselves. A world filled with awe and surprise and the knowledge that God is loving you in all of those places: in the asking, in the searching, in the willingness to knock on the unopened door. Jesus came to tell us that.

STEP BY STEP

Your thoughts ...

Blessed are you, pilgrim, if on the way you meet yourself and gift yourself with time, without rushing, so as not to disregard the image in your heart. ~ Beatitudes of the pilgrim

Day 11

My Beloved Soul

Will you ever trust that I am taking care of you?

When your thoughts run wildly into fearful places and your prayers seem weak and not at all worthwhile.

When you are not yourself and wonder where that person went.

When your worries overwhelm you and your readings seem to bring no comfort.

Remember that in all of those places of darkness my gentle voice is whispering words of comfort. Go into the quiet and you will hear me and know I am taking care of you. No matter how your feelings trick you, trying to make you believe you are apart from me, they are lies. You are my beloved soul. Always and everywhere.

"The Lord is my light and my salvation, whom should I fear? The Lord is my life's refuge; of whom should I be afraid?"

STEP BY STEP

Your thoughts ...

"Though an army encamp against me, my heart will not fear. Though war be waged upon me, even then will I trust." Psalm 27: 1, 3

Day 12

"I repeat, it is owing to his favor that salvation is yours through faith. This is not your own doing, it is God's gift, neither is it a reward for anything you have accomplished, so let no one pride himself on it. We are truly his handiwork, created in Christ Jesus to lead the life of good deeds which God prepared for us in advance." ~ Ephesians 2: 8-10

... "created in Christ Jesus to lead a life of good deeds." Today those good deeds are sometimes called "random acts of kindness." But what we call them matters not. Those deeds are magical and grand and holy. When someone waiting in line before you pays your bill, that simple but thoughtful deed has shown you the handiwork of the divine. And suddenly your cup of coffee becomes a spiritual experience - An ordinary day no more.

Maybe even an alleluia moment!

STEP BY STEP

Your thoughts ...

Blessed are you, pilgrim, if you see the handiwork of the Divine on this Camino.

Day 13

O Lord my God, prepare my spirit so that, through the intercession of the Apostle James, it may be open to your word, receive it, and put it into practice. Amen

May flowers spring up where your feet touch the earth.
May the feet that walked before you bless your every step.
May the weather that's important be the weather of your heart.
May all of your intentions find their way into the heart of God.
May your prayers be like flowers strewn for other pilgrims.
May your heart find meaning in unexpected events.
May friends who are praying for you carry you along the way.
May friends who are praying for you be carried in your heart.
May the circle of life encircle you along the way.
May the broken world ride on your shoulders.
May you carry your joy and your grief in the backpack of your soul.
May you remember all the circles of prayer throughout the world.
~Macrina Wiederkehr

STEP BY STEP

Your thoughts ...

Blessed are you, pilgrim, if you walk in prayer on this prayerful path.

Day 14

"My brothers, what is it to profess faith without practicing it? Such faith has no power to save one, has it? If a brother or sister has nothing to wear and no food for the day, and you say to them, "Good-bye and good luck! Keep warm and well fed," but do not meet their bodily needs, what good is that? So it is with the faith that does nothing in practice. It is thoroughly lifeless." ~ James 2:14-17

James wastes no words here. Are we active participants in our faith life? Or are we afraid to show up? Are we afraid that we are less than those around us and have nothing to offer? Remember God is as supremely happy with the one of quiet faith as he is with the missionary. When we choose the adventure and suspense of growing up spiritually. We are people of courage, people of a faith in God, alive and well.

STEP BY STEP

Your thoughts ...

Blessed are you, pilgrim, if you practice your faith.

Day 15

"So let us confidently approach the throne of grace to receive mercy and favor and to find help in time of need." ~ Hebrews 4:16

When we feel called by God to a certain task and want to move forward eagerly, sometimes it's important to wait. That waiting time is our time to step away from ourselves and pray for discernment.

If we can trust and be patient during this waiting time, and *"confidently approach the throne of grace to receive mercy and favor,"* then we need to believe that our lives will be serving up the answers we need. We will either be inspired to tackle the task or we will leave it for someone else to bring to life. It is not ours to do. Trust that God has other plans: something bigger, something better and something more our style.

STEP BY STEP

Your thoughts ...

Blessed are you, pilgrim, if you trust in God along this Camino and find this time for prayer and discernment.

Day 16

Jesus spoke to them once again; "I am the light of the world. No follower of mine shall ever walk in darkness; no, he shall possess the light of life." ~ John 8:12

When you are feeling unsettled, unlike yourself and in a strange land of your being, think of this. Think of the child inside you, the one who once needed a helping hand to cross the street. Sometimes these unsettled feelings signal a crossroad about to appear in your life. Kneel down and become that little child again. Reach for the Father's hand. Stop what you are doing or thinking and pray. Look outside yourself at the world awaiting you and pray. Listen to the quiet. It is only there that you will hear the voice of God. Feel the strength of knowing God is giving you courage. And know that being unsettled is not always a bad thing. Something good is happening. Something new is beginning to bloom. Be brave, be patient, be okay. And don't let go of the Father's hand. He will lead you out of the darkness so that you may "possess the light of life."

STEP BY STEP

Your thoughts ...

Blessed are you, pilgrim, when you hold our Father's hand. Listen to the quiet and know He is guiding you.

Day 17

"The Lord is my shepherd, I shall not want. In verdant pastures he gives me repose: Beside restful waters he leads me, he refreshes my soul ... He guides me on right paths for his names sake ... " ~ Psalm 23:1-3

Where was David in his life when he wrote his comforting and beautiful 23rd Psalm? What was going on around him that brought forth such words confirming the Lord's goodness?

Like us, was David feeling some kind of anxiety? Was he struggling because the ground under his feet felt unsteady? Perhaps he was hurting and needed reassurance and consolation. Whatever the reasons, God had mercy on him and on us, inspiring David to write these words. Words that throughout the ages, have given us a vision of the nurturing God, the good shepherd. The God who leads us beside restful waters, the one who guides us on right paths, the God who refreshes our soul.

Thank you, David, for sitting down and writing the glorious 23rd Psalm.

STEP BY STEP

Your thoughts ...

Blessed are you, pilgrim, when you allow God to refresh your soul along this journey.

Day 18

"Awake! Why are you asleep, O Lord? Arise! Cast us not off forever! Why do you hide your face, forgetting our woe and our oppression? For our souls are bowed down to the dust, our bodies are pressed to the earth. Arise, help us! Redeem us for your kindness' sake." ~ Psalm 44: 24-27

You are quiet, Lord. And I am not. My mind is full of constant chatter. I am filled with questions. And you are quiet. My prayers are as scattered as I am. To forgive looms large. I need your help. Yet I don't want it. Because it will mean I must forget the hurt, put aside the pain and forgive the enemy. Yes, I know I am stuck. Yes, I know this situation is holding me hostage Yes. Yes. Yes. And you, Lord, are quiet. Yet I know and I believe what Thomas Merton has written is true. *"You will never leave me to face my perils alone."* Help me, Lord, to free myself from one of the devil's most popular traps. Poor pitiful me!!! And there it is again, Lord. Die to self, die to self, die to self! I guess you are not asleep, Lord. You are not hiding from me. You are not at all quiet!

STEP BY STEP

Your thoughts ...

Blessed are you, pilgrim, if you die to self and trust in the Lord.

Day 19

"Only in God is my soul at rest; from him comes my salvation. He only is my rock and my salvation, my stronghold, I shall not be disturbed at all." ~Psalm 62: 1-3

Sometimes, Lord, I feel sorry for my little soul. Here I am full of my doubts and fears - disturbances for sure - and my poor soul has to deal with it all. I often wonder if my soul's wish is to be somewhere else, somewhere a little more calm and serene? Maybe in a monastery or a cloister? But you and I know it cannot be. You and I know those disturbances are part of my spiritual life's work.

Lord, help me to slow down, help me to sit in the quiet with you, for only there will my soul, my very self, find peace and rest. There with you, my rock and my stronghold, "I shall not be disturbed at all." Amen

STEP BY STEP

Your thoughts ...

Blessed are you, pilgrim, if you slow down on this Camino and find rest. Rest for your soul.

Day 20

"If today you hear his voice, harden not your hearts." ~ Psalm 95

Each of us is so different. And because of those differences, God's voice speaks to each one of us in our own special language. One may hear Him in a love for creation, another in the bonds of friendship, and still others hear Him in the language of art and music. But however we hear Him, and when we do, God has found us and we have found Him. Our hearts have been touched. Our soul refreshed. In that way, we are not so very different at all.

STEP BY STEP

Your thoughts ...

Blessed are you, pilgrim, if you hear His voice today.

Day 21

"He said to me, My grace is enough for you, for in weakness, power reaches perfection." ~ 2 Corinthians 12:9

Anxiety has always been my weak spot. And fear follows those feelings like a magnet. Or is it the other way around? First the fear, then the anxiety. Oh well, whatever the lineup, it is only grace that has carried me through and yes, sometimes into a feeling of power. Fighting our personal demons is a battle we fight with prayer on the forefront. And that prayer and God's grace has brought insight and for me removed the feelings of powerlessness - a popular sidekick of anxiety and panic. Is God's grace enough in order for us to fight those battles? I say yes. Because God's grace comes in so many shapes and sizes. What leads you to the right person to talk with, or the right meds that suit you perfectly, or the right book at the right time? God's grace. And what brought forth from me, who always seemed so fine, the courage to admit I am not okay. God's grace. God's grace. God's grace. I am so indebted to God's surprising grace.

STEP BY STEP

Your thoughts ...

Blessed are you, pilgrim, when you find God's grace on this path of life.

Day 22

"Merciful and gracious is the Lord, slow to anger and abounding in kindness." ~ Psalm 103

Of all the apostolates open to all of us, the most effective, the most far-reaching, the most consoling is Kindness.

Kindness is one of God's best gifts to the world. It drives gloom and darkness from souls. It puts hope into fainting hearts. It sweetens sorrow. It lessens pain. It discovers unsuspected beauties of human character.

It calls forth a response from all that is best in souls. It purifies, glorifies, gathers the tears of repentant love. It lightens the burden of weariness. It stops the torrent of angry passion. It takes the sting from failure. It kindles courageous ambition. It lifts the unfortunate. It leads back the wayward. It walks in the steps of our Savior.

Let us become apostles of Kindness, to partake of its sweetness, to aspire to its holiness. The apostolate of Kindness is exalted; it is sublime; it is Christlike.

Author Unknown

STEP BY STEP

Your thoughts ...

Blessed are you, pilgrim, when you show kindness to others.

Day 23

My Beloved Soul

Relax. I am with you. You may not feel my presence, but your feelings are not always the truth. The truth is that I am never apart from you. The truth is that feelings come and go; put no trust in them. Stay with your prayers. Let them flow, and they will bring you out of the darkness. My way, My truth, My light is yours, no matter your feelings.

"Again Jesus spoke to them, saying, "I am the light of the world. Whoever follows me will not walk in darkness, but will have the light of life." - John 8:12

STEP BY STEP

Your thoughts ...

Blessed are you pilgrim, if you discover that the "camino" holds a lot of silence; and the silence of prayer; and the prayer of meeting with God who is waiting for you. ~ Beatitudes of the pilgrim

Day 24

"This is another day, O Lord. If I am to stand up, help me to stand bravely. If I am to sit still, help me to sit quietly. If I am to lie low, help me to do it patiently. And if I am to do nothing, let me do it gallantly." ~ Book of Common Prayer

Doing Nothing

> *Some of us need to discover that we will not begin to live more fully until we have the courage to do and see and taste and experience much less than usual.*
>
> *There are times then, when in order to keep ourselves in existence at all, we simply have to sit back for a while and do nothing. And for the man who has let himself be drawn completely out of himself by his activity, nothing is more difficult than to sit still and rest, doing nothing at all.*
>
> *The very act of resting is the hardest and most courageous act he can perform.* ~ Thomas Merton

STEP BY STEP

Your thoughts ...

Blessed are you, pilgrim, if you can walk along this Camino completely out of yourself and doing nothing at all.

Day 25

"You are the light of the world. A city set on a hill cannot be hidden. Men do not light a lamp and then put it under a bushel basket. They set it on a stand where it gives light to all in the house. In the same way, your light must shine before men so that they may see the goodness in your acts and give praise to your heavenly father." ~Matthew 5:14-16

First and foremost, we must accept that we are good. If we are made in the image and likeness of God and God is love, how can we not be good? As long as we keep judging ourselves and putting our talented spirits in the jail of our own making, we imprison our true self. Free yourselves to be all that God intended you to be. Trust yourself to step out into the dream God has for you. When you were born you were given everything you needed to fulfill God's plan for you. Step out and let your light shine.

STEP BY STEP

Your thoughts ...

Blessed are you, pilgrim, if you free yourself along this Camino.

Day 26

"A nice definition of an awakened person: a person who no longer marches to the drums of society, a person who dances to the tune of the music that springs from within." ~ Fr. Anthony DeMello

Lord, is my music being heard?

Are my dancing steps a challenge?

Am I awake to the songs you send me on an ordinary day?

STEP BY STEP

Your thoughts ...

Blessed are you, pilgrim, if you hear the music from within.

Day 27

"True religion is real living; living with all one's soul, with all one's goodness and righteousness." ~ Albert Einstein

Living with all one's soul

The little personality given to us at our birth wants many things. The lovely soul who joined us there, wants only one thing. And that one thing is that the soul and the personality will joyfully journey together, walk hand in hand to become the one formed by God in our mother's womb.

The soul and the self will take this journey in a partnership unlike any other. The vocal self wants what it wants, but the silent soul knows the spiritual needs of it's distracted human self. The soul knows about the power of grace and the power of the Spirit waiting patiently to help us find our way to God. And so, the soul never loses hope that the personality will awake to its inner needs. And when wakefulness comes, the mercy of God is blinding.

STEP BY STEP

Your thoughts ...

Blessed are you, pilgrim, when wakefulness comes.

Day 28

"Anyone who listens to the Word and takes no action is like someone who looks at his own features in a mirror and, once he has seen what he looks like, goes off and immediately forgets it. But anyone who looks steadily at the perfect law of freedom and keeps to it, not listening and forgetting, but putting it into practice, will be blessed in every undertaking." ~ James 1:22-25

Here James gives us simple rules for finding blessing in our lives. One, listen to the Word. Two, don't forget it and three, put it into practice. Then another, just as important, keep the perfect law of freedom!! Because if we have burdened ourselves with rules to follow, our anxious thinking will silence the voice of God. Listening to the Word needs a quiet mind. In that quiet, the Spirit will lead us to our gifts and make us ready to take God's work for us out and into the world. Be brave, speak through your gifts, and then prepare yourself to be "blessed in every undertaking."

STEP BY STEP

Your thoughts ...

Blessed are you, pilgrim, if you allow the Spirit to guide you to your gifts.

Day 29

"Life is everything. Life is God. Everything changes and moves and that movement is God. And while there is life there is joy in consciousness of the divine. To love life is to love God." ~ Leo Tolstoy

I tried very hard to write something that would enlighten us about this quote. All I can say after sitting with Mr. Tolstoy's words is, "what was I thinking?"

I could never be inspired beyond what was given to him and to him only. His holy words are a pure blessing to read.

> *"Life is everything. Life is God. Everything changes and moves and that movement is God. And while there is life there is joy in consciousness of the divine. To love life is to love God."*

All I dare to say is "Amen."

STEP BY STEP

Your thoughts ...

Blessed are you, pilgrim, if you love life.

Day 30

"The Spirit God has given us is no cowardly spirit, but rather one that makes us strong, loving and wise" ~2 Timothy 1:7

Wouldn't it be wonderful if we never doubted those words; if we could believe firmly in the power of those gifts and be strengthened by them. But it seems in times of deep need, when we long to believe in those promises the most, the devil of doubt sets up home inside our spirit. Despair looms large. We have no strength, we have no wisdom, and love is something for better times. As some might say, we have lost our "mojo." But really, we have lost our faith in knowing God's spirit and grace is working in us. If who you are and why you are have come apart, don't despair. "God has given us no cowardly spirit." Trust in the presence of His grace - one moment at a time, one day at a time, one prayer at a time.

STEP BY STEP

Your thoughts ...

Blessed are you, pilgrim, if you trust in the presence of His grace.

Day 31

"Explore daily the will of God." ~ C.G Jung

And don't be surprised if, in your daily explorations, you find yourself asking God hard questions. Don't be shy. Ask away. God is in this place of unsteadiness with you. Lean on him and be calm. His angels are accompanying you. Be patient. God will give you as much time as you need to explore his will for your life. Enjoy the journey. Be courageous. Practice trusting in Him.

In his poem, "Patient Trust in Ourselves and in the Slow Work of God," Pierre Teilhard de Chardin says this:

> *"Only God could say what this new spirit gradually forming within you will be. Give our Lord the benefit of believing that his hand is leading you, and accept the anxiety of feeling yourself in suspense and incomplete."*

STEP BY STEP

Your thoughts ...

"Please show me your Divine Will in this matter and send a clear sign that gives the proper direction. And if for some reason I'm about to head the wrong way, please, please stop me." ~ Tosha Silver, Outrageous Openness: Letting the Divine Take the Lead

Day 32

"At times all we do is to utter a word with all our heart, yet it is as if we lifted up a whole world. It is as if someone unsuspectingly pressed a button and a gigantic wheel-work were stormily and surprisingly set in motion." ~
Rabbi Joshua Herschel

When we feel powerless, when our hurt and pain want to overcome us and God seems far away, we cannot forget the power of prayer. It is in that place of weakness, that Rabbi Herschel encourages us to pray; *"Utter a word with all your heart, yet it is as if we lifted up a whole world."* Maybe you won't feel like you have lifted up a whole world, but if I know our God, he will have lifted up *your* world.

Sometime, somewhere, I read these words: *"even the mere inclination to pray is prayer itself."* I may not remember the author, but I did not forget his message. Nor will I forget Rabbi Herschel. These are the encouraging words of those who are a little ahead of us on our journey of faith. I thank God for all of those spiritual mentors he surprises us with on our curvy and bumpy spiritual path.

STEP BY STEP

Your thoughts ...

Blessed are you, pilgrim, if you utter a word with all your heart.

Day 33

Let Your God Love You

Be silent.
Be still.
Alone.

Empty before your God.

Say nothing.
Ask nothing.
Be silent.
Be still.

Let your God look upon you.

That is all.

God knows and understands.
God loves you with an enormous love,

Quiet.
Still.
Be.
Let your God love you.

~Edwina Gately

STEP BY STEP

Your thoughts ...

Blessed are you, pilgrim, because you have discovered that the true Camino begins at its end.

For those still walking ...

My Beloved Soul

I understand you. I see your heart, your soul, your spirit. And there is nothing you can do or say or not do that will separate me from you. My love is not like human love. It is not measured out and given according to your good deeds. Just by being you, one of my souls on the journey of life, means you are my beloved. I understand all that makes you the person you are. Love that person and let your light shine out and into my troubled world. Pray for a peaceful spirit.

"The Lord bless you and keep you! The Lord let his face shine upon you, and be gracious to you! The Lord look upon you kindly and give you peace." ~Numbers: 6: 24-26

STEP BY STEP

Your thoughts ...

"In every walk with Nature one receives far more than he seeks." ~ *John Muir*

Still walking ...

My Beloved Soul

If you draw yourself away from the world by the simple act of putting aside the things that call to be done and walk towards prayer time, heaven rejoices. Whether in silence or in words, you have joined the angels for that moment in time. Know that you need those moments, away and alone, with Me. Know that when you put aside the world for prayer time, you gain the grace and strength to live in the world. But remember too, that when I hear those prayers lifted in the middle of your busyness, the prayers that spring forth from your soul in those moments between moments, I rejoice in your faithful heart.

STEP BY STEP

Your thoughts ...

Prayer may not save us, but prayer makes us worth saving. ~ Abraham Joshua Heschel

Still walking ...

My Beloved Soul

When the mind is still, the soul breathes.

I want our quiet time together to refresh you. I want that silence to take you away from all that is tiring you, all that is distracting you, all that the world is wanting from you. Come into the quiet. Be still. Surrender your worries, your striving to figure things out, and let our quiet prayer time refresh you. Let your soul breathe you into my presence. I am here.

> *O Lord, my heart is not proud, nor are my eyes haughty; I busy not myself with great things, nor with things too sublime for me. Nay, rather I have stilled and quieted my soul like a weaned child. Like a weaned child on its mother's lap, (so is my soul within me) Psalm 131: l-2*

STEP BY STEP

Your thoughts ...

"Half an hour's meditation each day is essential, except when you are busy. Then a full hour is needed." ~ Saint Francis de Sales

Reflect ...

"There is only one thing that makes a dream impossible to achieve: the fear of failure." ~ Paulo Coelho

STEP BY STEP

Reflect ...

"Some journeys take us far from home. Some adventures lead us to our destiny." ~ C.S. Lewis

Reflect ...

"The secret of happiness is to live moment by moment and to thank God for all that He, in His goodness, sends to us day after day." ~ *St. Gianna Molla*

STEP BY STEP

Reflect ...

"Nothing great is ever achieved without enduring much." ~ St. Catherine of Siena

Your journey home ...

A pilgrim's journey is a round trip. It really begins when we return home.

In the story of the Transfiguration on Mount Tabor, the disciples wish to remain with Christ in his glory a little bit longer. Peter says, "If you wish, I will make three tents here," Matt 17:4. Yet Jesus leads Peter, James, and John back down the mountain.

The same applies to your pilgrimage experience. I know we all want to stay in this holy place, and you are probably already planning when you can do this again. But the time has come. It is time to leave and return home.

Here are some prayers for the "journey down the mountain."

May you look forward to the great things that will come next after your mountaintop experience.

STEP BY STEP

Prayer to Walk the Path of the Beatitudes

Heavenly Father, we have gone up "to the heights" as your servant, Pier Giorgio Frassati, once did in the mountains of Turin.

We have experienced transformation and joy, and now we continue on our way into the valleys of life, walking the way of the Beatitudes in all we say and do.

Give us the strength, Lord, to follow Pier Giorgio's example: To lift up the poor in spirit, to comfort those who mourn; To be simple and meek, to hunger and thirst for justice; To be merciful and compassionate, to be pure in heart; To be a peacemaker, to stand with courage in persecution.

As we make our way down from the mountaintop, may we live as he lived, and transform our world. We ask this through Christ our Lord. Amen.

Blessed Pier Giorgio Frassati, man of the beatitudes, patron of young adults, and lover of the mountains, is an inspiration for all people of faith. We pray through his intercession for the strength to live out the path of the beatitudes in daily life.
© 2015 United States Conference of Catholic Bishops. Washington, D.C. All rights reserved.

Your journey home ...

"What is broken can be mended. What hurts can be healed. And no matter how hard it gets, the sun will rise again." ~ **Unknown**

STEP BY STEP

Your journey home ...

"The best journeys answer questions that in the beginning you didn't even think to ask."
 ~ Jeff Johnson

Made in the USA
Las Vegas, NV
02 December 2022

60979006R00062